AF505762

A JOURNEY TO CALIFORNIA IN 1849

A JOURNEY
TO CALIFORNIA
IN 1849

By W. C. S. SMITH

Facsimile of the 1925 (?) Napa, California title page.

A JOURNEY
TO CALIFORNIA
IN 1849

BY

WILLIAM C.S. SMITH

YE GALLEON PRESS
FAIRFIELD, WASHINGTON

Library of Congress Cataloging in Publication Data

Smith, William C. S., 1823-
    A journey to California in 1849.

    Reprint.
    Includes index.
    1. California—Description and travel—1848-1869. 2. California-
Gold discoveries.   3. Overland journeys to the Pacific.   4.
Mexico—Description and travel. 5. Smith, William C.S., 1823- I. Title.
F 865.S7   1984   979.4'04   84-12000
ISBN o-87770-327-2

BIOGRAPHICAL NOTES

William C.S. Smith was born in Franklin, Warren County, Ohio, in 1823. He moved to Muscatine County, Iowa, in 1840, and to New York City in 1848. January 15, 1849, he started for California, coming via Vera Cruz, City of Mexico, San Blas and Mazatlan to Cape Saint Lucas, and thence by land to San Diego, where he arrived June 10th of that year, and thence to San Francisco, arriving July 6th following. He proceeded at once to the mines at Ross Bar, on the Yuba River, where he engaged in that occupation for a while. He then proceeded to Slate Range, opposite the mouth of Slate Creek, where he spent the remainder of the summer. That fall he went to Sacramento, and ran a boat to Nyes Landing, now Marysville. During the winter of 1849 he established a mercantile house at Marysville, with several branch houses in the mountains. In 1852 he purchased a tract of land in Napa Valley from Salvador Vallejo, and in 1853 moved upon it. April 14, 1865, he was appointed by President Lincoln to the position of Collector of Internal Revenue of the Fifth District of California. This appointment was made the day before the assassination of President Lincoln, and the signing of the document was his last official act. Mr. Smith filled the position with honor and fidelity for twelve years, and until the Fifth District was merged with the Fourth. Upon retiring his accounts were examined by the Treasury Department and found to be correct in every particular. He is now engaged in the retail grocery business in Napa City. While it can not be said of Mr. Smith that he has gotten unto himself a great name, yet the nobler praise is due him of having always done what his hands found to do, with a conscientious regard for truth, honor and fidelity. He has always taken an active part in the advancement of all that tends to the moral and social as well as the financial advancement of the city in which he resides. He was married March 4, 1858, to Miss Margaret J. Hornbeck, who died July 21, 1869, leaving four children: Jeanetta A., Charles G., Egbert T., and William T. In 1870 he married, secondly, Mrs. Alice Hinckley.

Biographical material reprinted courtesy Slocum, Bowen and Co., Publishers, San Francisco, California, 1881.

A JOURNEY TO CALIFORNIA

IN 1849

January 15th, 1849 — To me a day "big with fate." I sailed from New York on the barque *Eugenia* bound for California. A land at that time teeming with mysterious hope and doubt. I was a stranger. Not one person aboard that I had known forty-eight hours. My uncle and cousins bade me good-bye as if forever. The day was dark and gloomy. The bay filled with floating ice. Thoughts of years crowded into each moment as we glided swiftly down the bay. Just as the sun went down we passed the Hook. The tug cast us off and now for the first time I was on the heaving ocean.

Directly a furious northeaster, with snow and sleet, struck us. Some peculiar sensations, perhaps not worth mentioning — yet well remembered — compelled me to make a dive below in concert with my 106 fellow sufferers. Oh! Horror! What a night. Our quarters filled full of all kinds of baggage. Hatches closed. No light. All seasick, and the vessel pitching and plunging every way.

But let that pass as an oft-told tale. Suffice it, we soon ran into the Gulf Stream and pleasant weather. The rest of the voyage was rapid and delightful. The evening of January the 29th we sighted the land of Mexico, the peak of Orizaba showing right on the face of the sun, and on the 30th we anchored in the harbor of Vera Cruz, within a stone's throw of the castle of San Juan de Ulloa.

Vera Cruz, with its fortifications, white walls, flat roofs, dark-skinned population and turkey buzzards, had a novel appearance to one so untraveled. It required no effort of imagination to realize that this was really the Sunny South. To our northern constitutions the heat was almost intollerable. I did not know or wish to know where the thermometer stood, but felt in very desperation that between the red flannel and woolen clothes (which we all wore to "keep off yellow fever" by advice of those returned from the late war) and the effect of the scorching sun we would surely dissolve, unless, fortunately, we should dry up into the shrivelled, mummy-like condition of many of the inhabitants. By the way, we were told that as a general thing they do not die, but gradually dry up and blow away. I cannot vouch for this as a fact. though it seems possible.

On the 2nd of February our company, consisting of eight or ten Vermonters, three Frenchmen, a lot of broken merchants from New York, Gardner, Nye and myself (the only western man), in all 21 persons, took up a line of march under the command of Captain M. Our captain was a man utterly ignorant of anything practical apart from the work of a counting house. He was chosen on account of a report that he was in some way allied to a certain great shipping house in New York. His self-esteem was immense. The brave captain said himself that no other man with us was as well qualified to conduct us through the hostile country that lay before us! In fact he seemed to feel that the mantle of General Scott had fallen upon him, and that under his command we were to hew a bloody path across poor Mexico. Upon the country fellow, and especially upon me, a western clod-hopper he looked far down with peculiar disdain, but I was not afraid of his kind.

Our caravan in "tout ensemble" was unique. In the van bestride a tall war steed rode our brave commander, his broadsword girded to his side, with one hand vigorously grasping the pommel of his saddle. Slightly in the rear, similarly accoutered with the addition of a huge pair of jingling silver-plated spurs, moved Lieutenant B. After our leaders came a number of the city nobs, also mounted. Then followed the wagons, two old baggage wains left by the army and rigged up after the design of our worthy lieutenant in the following style:

To each was attached by ropes, chains, thongs of rawhide and old artillery harness, with traces about 15 feet long, seven lean, lanky, half-starved but vicious mules; first two on the pole, on one of which was mounted a half naked, swarthy greaser, almost hidden by a huge, broad-brimmed, steeple crowned hat. Then came three more mules abreast, and then two on the lead, the last selected as being the most miserable and easiest knocked down. This operation being occasionally necessary to stop the wagon on a down grade as there were neither brakes or hold-back fixtures of any kind. In the rear of the wagons was marshalled on foot a dozen or more of us common fellows, the remainder of the band. We stood in double file, armed to the teeth with about all weapons known in modern warfare.

In this order after much ordering, kicking of mules and cajoling we got started and marched out of the western gate of the city as the sun was going down. By moonlight we ploughed our way through the sand six miles to our first camp. Here the privates of the company were told off into two watches to stand guard alternately through the night, and I was honored with an appointment as sergeant of the watch. Our able commander instructed me to make regular rounds to each picket during the night and see that the guards were awake and vigilant, and then he went to his tent to sleep. Deeply impressed with the grave responsibilty resting upon me in this my first military office, I was green enough to obey to the letter, spending the night in discovering imaginery guerrillas in each bush on the sandhills and, with the assistance of my brave comrades, was able to hold our dangerous post until morning. When we broke camp it was raining and, by special order, we lumbered on without breakfast—which dampened our ardor and caused some growling.

It was found necessary that the snobs should assist the mules. So we just pushed up every hill all day, and nearly all the road was uphill. In one desperate struggle a wagon tongue was broken. A council of war was held and, under the supervision of our great chief, the tongue was spliced — and such a splice!

We made Santa Fe at noon, where we dined on what the boys pronounced jackass meat. But hunger is a good sauce. It needed to be in that case. We camped early at a small ranch on account of the broken tongue. The captain decided to send back to Vera Cruz for another. I volunteered to fix it in half an hour better than it ever was and did what any farmer would have done at first. The tongue was five feet longer than the little mules. I had with me a hatchet, augur bits and saw and soon set it back and bolted it in the hounds. And from that time was regularly installed wagon mender and greaser. Someone had told the captain that wagon wheels needed grease. He was surprised.

In our company were some real good fellows — gentlemen in the true meaning of that word. A word often misapplied, but never by one who has had the experience of such a trip as mine. Three or four of my companions were men I can never forget. Men of that stamp whose character develops and rises when actual difficulties and dangers come. Quiet, yet energetic and brave; pleasant in manner but firm; self-denying and generous at all times and under all circumstances from first to last; always the same. Nature's noblemen — true gentlemen.

It was only by degrees I learned the character of my associates. I being a kind of an off-side ox — a stranger to them all. When difficulties came, then, and not until then, did we understand each other. In time of trouble one soon learns who to trust and who to shun. It certainly did need some good alloy to give our company a decent average, for we surely had with us some of the meanest, most selfish and cowardly puppies that could be produced anywhere. Especially so after their Broadway airs and swagger had departed.

In six days' march from the "Tierra Caliente" to the "Tierra Templada" by dint of beating the mules and pushing the wagons we reached Jalapa. Our route was by the National Road. We noticed with interest many traces and relics of the war, particularly at the National Bridge and the battle ground of Cerro Gordo. The whole distance our aristocratic members stuck to the horses, which were company property, bought from a joint fund, while we more humble followers trudged along with sore feet and weary limbs; but that is all right. It was a long lane, and it is my recollection that we paid them off well before they saw the Pacific.

Jalapa is a beautiful place. There is nothing striking in the architecture of these Mexican towns. Their dead walls and flat roofs are monotonous, but the situation, climate and surroundings of Jalapa are delightful, especially to one coming from the hot region below. The elevation is at just a happy mean between heat and frost. The town is situated in a sort of amphitheater among the mountains and is quite embowered in orange, lemon, banana and many other tropical plants and trees—all new and strange to me. The air was delightfully fragrant with the perfume of gorgeous flowers. Mexicans are proud of Jalapa. Here one of the company, a very worthy young fellow by the name of Broughton, was accidentally shot in the thigh. The ball was extracted by our surgeon and we made him as comfortable as possible, but contrary to the general wish, by order we went on and left him the day after the accident. Blake, who shot him, properly remained to care for him. Afterwards they overtook us at Guadalajara, traveling by litter and diligence.

We left Jalapa all well mounted. Traveling about thirty

miles a day. We passed in succession La Hoya, Las Vegas, Perote, with its gloomy castle prison, and many other small towns to the great City of Puebla. Leaving Jalapa the National Road winds around and up a mountainside, until we reached an elevated plateau from 8,000 to 9,000 feet above the sea. Except an occasional barranca, our road lay at such height. This entire tableland from Jalapa to Puebla is based upon a porous volcanic rock. There are few wells or springs. The rivers flow in chasms 1,000 or 2,000 feet in depth, with perpendicular sides, apparently as riven asunder by earthquakes. The most of these barancas are crossed by solid stone arched bridges built by the old Spanish government. Several of these bridges were blown up to stop our army, but our engineers cut graded roads down the rock face of the barancas and the army passed over. I doubt if they are ever rebuilt by Mexicans.

The extreme rarity of the atmosphere caused our lips and noses to bleed so that they became very sore.

Orizaba had loomed above us many days. It was always in sight from the first view at sea—a beautiful, white, snow-clad pyramid of perfect symmetry—until the day before reaching Puebla, when we passed around the base of the more lofty Popocatapetl and lost sight of the beautiful peak. We stopped in Puebla but a few hours, but long enough to observe that it is a large and populous city. The cathedral is an immense structure. We examined its exterior with admiration and regretted that time would not permit us to see the interior and the celebrated solid silver altar rail said to be worth millions of dollars.

By the time we had reached this place our noble captain and our chivalrous lieutenant had succeeded in creating a miserable feeling of jealous discord in the company. Each of the gentlemen impressed with the honors due to their high official positions became offended with each other because of some slight omissions or breaches of military etiquette. Savage words were spoken and bloody threats were made. Each had their supporters. Some of us on the outside had a hope they would be as good as their bloody talk—but they were both cowards. It was all smoke. There were three elements in the personnel of our party, viz: The Vermonters and New Yorkers, the captain's original company; six Frenchmen and, thirdly, three volunteers who had joined on the ship, namely, Dan Gardner (a brother of President Tyler's wife), William F. Nye (a son of Captain Ezra Nye of the Collins S. Ship Pacific) and myself. The lieutenant was leader of the Frenchmen. We three went it alone and held the balance. Soon several of the Vermonters and Frenchmen joined with us in a league offensive and defensive and thereafter we had comparative peace.

About three miles west of Puebla we passed near the great Pyramid of Cholula. I remember that while we were viewing the pyramid with interest and about to ascend it, it was announced that one of the miserable old wagons had broken down and we were wanted in haste to make repairs. So I did not ascend Cholula.

Thence to the City of Mexico the country is a rough, broken table land, 8,000 feet or more above the sea, and too cold for tropical vegetation. Everywhere one sees the century plant, or maguey, from which pulque, the national drink is made. We northerners call it century plant from the long time it takes to bloom in our hot houses. Here it blooms and dies in two or three years, but constantly renews itself from sprouts. When in blossom, the natives cut off the central stock and scoop out a cavity in the stump from which each morning they dip several gallons of juice. With this juice they fill the whole skin of a hog and hang it from a tree. In two or three days it ferments and becomes pulque. Then they draw it off from a leg, drink it and get very drunk. We saw the whole process as we journeyed along. We could not imagine how anyone could drink the stuff. To our taste it was offensive.

The approach to the City of Mexico is over a long causeway between shallow lakes and marshes. The city is built upon a low, flat island which is only a few inches above the water, and from which causeways radiate like the spokes of a wheel. Occasional bridges permit canoe navigation by channels across the causeways from one lake to another. It is not unusual for the city to be flooded. There is no outlet to these lakes or from the Valley of Mexico. As a result of this want of drainage there is much malarial disease, although the altitude is about 7,000 feet. A large part of the city is said to be built upon land reclaimed from the marsh.

We remained here four days. I visited the great cathedral, the museum and state house. Saw the equestrian statue in bronze, 25 feet high, of Charles the something—I forget—of Spain, the iron armor of Cortez and feather armor of Montezuma, the celebrated calendar and sacrificial stones and many other interesting relics of the Aztecs and Spanish conquerors; walked through the Bazaar and Alameda, had my pocket picked and got a general insight into everything around. The majority of the population are apparently Indians or worse mongrel half-breeds, and the latter we then and afterwards found to our sorrow are most adroit thieves.

We put up at the Hotel de Paris, a large, three-story maison. Like most of the better class of houses it is built in a quadrangle with an open court in the center in the middle of which was a playing fountain, a water tank, plants and blooming flowers. The street walls have but one opening, an archway from the court closed by iron gates. The ground floor was occupied by the officers and stables, accomodation for all kinds of bipeds from men to chickens being above.

On leaving we passed out the northern gate. Had a distant

view of Chapultepec. Myriads of wild geese and ducks arose from the ponds and marshes on either side of the road.

Our next objective point was Queratro, by the way of Tula, which we made in some six days of difficult travel, the wagons giving us much trouble. In one downhill rush a wagon capsized and, with mules and all, rolled over several times. Queratro is a large town. We were impressed with the novel small currency in use, viz., small cakes of dirty white soap, and supposed here might be the origin of the phrase, "How are you off for soap."

While here we had many and full reports of an organized band of robbers who were waiting ahead with the avowed intention of capturing our company. Accordingly our valiant captain detailed a detachment of five scouts (in which I had the honor to serve) who were instructed to beat up the thickets and ravines on each side and in advance of the main body. Sensible that our orders were from a master in military strategy we undertook the duty with ardor. Volumes only could tell of feats performed in the way of scaling barancas, leaping cactus hedges and not least in visiting hospitable haciendas off the road. After three days' active service without the capture of one ladrone, we fell back and resumed the usual order of march. By the way, my impression is that it was not a good time for guerrillas or they would surely have caught us. But we had a good lark and a free, jolly time away from the cares of the train and bullying of our noble captain.

At Lagos, Miller and some others overtook and joined our party. Between Queratro and Guadalajara we passed through several populous towns, whose people were not civil or friendly, as we had found them to be so far as our army had advanced.

Guadalajara is a city of 60,000 or 70,000 inhabitants. Has many fine public and private buildings and apparently does more manufacturing than any other place we saw in Mexico.

We found the place preeminently infested with thieves. Few of us left there with a handkerchief or any article carried in a pocket. This is the terminus of the great Camino Real, or National Road. It had been arranged that here we would leave the wagons and pack through with mules; but our captain (some others assenting), fired with the idea of taking the first wagons to the Pacific shore, and by what was called an impracticable route for wheeled vehicles, and considering that the feat would redound to his fame when published in a New York paper of which he was a correspondent, determined to defy obstacles and force a way through the mountains—and it was done.

Soon after leaving Guadalajara all traces of a wagon road disappeared, leaving nothing but a mule trail, full of rocks and all kinds of impediments, through which for six days we worked a weary way to Tekela. From there on difficulties grew serious, and nothing but desperate exertion accomplished an undertaking which most of us had pronounced useless and foolhardy before commenced.

To relate all the incidents of that mountain journey, how we worked ourselves to the wagons like mules, the descent into the great baranca, a gorge of some 2000 feet in depth, with sides almost perpendicular, letting down the wagons in pieces by ropes; the labor of getting out of that dark, deep chasm, rolling stones to build roads, and even a partial description of that rugged travel would exceed the design of this rough sketch.

At San Lionel, with Nye and two others, I left the company at 12 o'clock one night and rode forward forty miles to Tepic, where we arrived in the early morning. Tepic is a pretty place—in location, climate and vegetation. It is much like Jalapa on the eastern slope.

Our attention was attracted by observing among the people an unusually large proportion of light complexions.

Apparently pure-blooded Castilians—a number of European families have their homes here. They are people connected with mercantile houses doing business through Pacific ports, and live here for health and comfort. We hired an "arriero" or packer and mules to pack our baggage, and at four o'clock the following morning mounted our horses for the last time, and rode off down the mountains for San Blas, distant seventy miles.

For the first ten or more miles the trail descended rapidly. In many places it was a narrow gutter worn in the soft chalk rock and so deep that we were forced to sit with our legs on the neck of the horse. We made a forced march.

We had heard there was a ship at San Blas about to sail for San Francisco, and we wanted to stop her for the benefit of our company, who were laboring on with the horrid old wagons.

From Jalapa I had ridden a splendid large gray horse. The entire journey he performed nobly, but that day's ride nearly finished him. Poor fellow! I was sorry to part with him. I sold him at San Blas to the kind-hearted hostess of the "Maison Guadalupe" who wanted him for her own use, and promised to take good care of him. But I am anticipating.

For about thirty miles the trail was rugged and constantly descending. The vegetation gradually becoming more luxuriant until presently the foot of the great western slope was reached and we were in a dense wilderness of tropical trees and plants. Banyan, cocoa palms and huge leaved banana trees arched overhead, forming a screen that almost obscured the path, but made the air delightfully cool and pleasant. We called one tree "Banyan," from a resemblance in growth to the tree of Indian.

Some of these trees had hundreds of supporting trunks, and after all we found it was a vine to a huge tree or rather grove. First, as a little vine it climbed the tall palms to the top, with many lateral branches growing around the tree and hugging like Laocoon serpents, presently these laterals unite in a solid growth of wood and the poor, doomed palm is all hidden, save a tuft of foliage at the lofty top; finally it is choked to death, decays and there remains a huge, hollow cylinder; from this other branching vines drop down and take root, climb adjacent trees, and so the work goes on.

We also noticed many wild coffee trees loaded with berries, and saw many large iguanas, a tree lizard which grows from three to five feet long, and are by the natives esteemed a delicate food.

One day some of us bought at a roadside place what we thought was cold fried veal, and splendid eating, until our interpreter told us, "Yes, it is very good, but it is not veal, it is lizard." We dropped it.

March 14 we reached San Blas after dark, quite tired out by our long ride. We turned in too weary to take a first look at the Pacific ocean, whose waves were booming nearby. I slept soundly notwithstanding a fandango in the next room.

Early in the morning we were rowed out to the Hawaiian barque *Mary Frances,* at anchor in the harbor a mile or more from shore, and secured passage on her to San Francisco. We then remained in San Blas three days. This place, probably because of it being one of the few harbors or roadsteads on the unindented west coast, is prominently marked on maps, and we were surprised to find it only a small village of low thatched houses built of mud and reeds. A large trade passes through this port, but the business houses representing the same are located in Tepic and other towns in the temperate interior. On the southern side of the town rising conspicuously above the level of the flat land and dense vegetation is an old, massive Spanish fortification. It is built upon an isolated rock, with a flat top of about an acre in area. Standing so alone and with perpendicular sides a hundred feet or more in height, one might imagine the rock had been shoved bodily up out of the plain.

At almost the last hour fixed for the ship to sail the poor boys came straggling in with the miserable old wagons. How they ever got them over the road was past understanding. The natives examined the wagons as curiosities—something they had not seen before.

While at this place some of our fellows got into a terrible and foolish row with the natives at a fandango. Four or five of the latter were killed and several of our company wounded, one desperately. A body of soldiers from the fort came in good time and hurried all of us Americans aboard the ship to save us from a mob of angry greasers who were anxious to cut our throats.

The *Mary Frances* was an old condemned whaler of some 400 tons. Had been sold to the King of the Sandwich Islands, who had used her as a play warship. He had heard of the great California migration and thought here was a chance to make money, and so sent the old tub down to carry a load of passengers. With no fixtures save the bare, oil soaked decks, old oil barrels for water tanks, and as a cooking range two try kettles in a furnace, just as left by the whalers—our quarters and food were both pretty rough. To each of us was allotted and marked on the main deck with chalk a space of about four by eight feet, where we were expected to keep all our belongings and to sleep. All around us was a herd of filthy greasers, who had scarce room to sit down. The cabin was monopolized by a wealthy Mexican signor and his family.

Six days' dull sailing and drifting brought us to Mazatlan. This harbor, though said to be unsafe for large vessels, being unprotected from westerly gales, has a fine appearance from the sea. The anchorage for ships is a mile or more from the town. several high, rocky islands stand around the entrance to the harbor. Behind one of these islands at the head of a shallow bay, hidden from view from the sea, lies the town.

Outside of us, near the mouth of the outer harbor, was anchored the fine English frigate *Constant,* said to be one of the finest men-of-war afloat. A boat from her in charge of a young officer boarded us as we anchored, and made a kind tender of assistance if needed. The officers of the *Constant* treated us Americans with much civility. We had a standing invitation to visit the ship and partake of refreshments.

Mazatlan is a city of some ten thousand inhabitants and probably is the most important seaport on the west coast of Mexico. A large part of its trade is smuggling off Mexican silver dollars to be used in China, Hawaii and at this time especially in California, where fourteen of these dollars buy an ounce of gold dust worth $21. Of course our captain was in the business deep. The export duty is heavy, and the customs officers must have big pay to keep out of sight.

Captain Paty thought these fellows were getting too large a percentage, and concluded to run off some dollars on the sly. He made a proposition to us Americans to help him. Six of us gladly accepted, as it promised to give us a jolly good time. Each morning we were sent ashore in the captain's boat, had carriages and drivers to visit around the city and country, a splendid dinner at "La Fonda Italliene," cigars, wine and fruit all free. In the afternoon we would one by one drop into Mott and Robinson's counting room and fill our pockets and hats with all the dollars we could pack secretly, stroll down to the shore, be rowed aboard, hand over the silver, and then have a fine supper in the captain's cabin.

This went on nicely for several days, when one evening as our boat was shoving off, we were startled by being surrounded by a file of soldiers with swords drawn over our heads. We were marched off and locked up in a dark prison, where we were kept until morning with no accommodation but a stone floor. Then we were taken before a court, searched and made to hand over the dollars and, after much talk, were allowed to go—and we went quickly, glad to get off so easy.

There was a high, rocky island between where our ship lay and the town. During the late war the sailors from one of the U.S. ships dragged several cannon up the steep sides of this rock to the top, and thus compelled the city and fort to surrender. One day some of us landed on this island and after a hard climb reached the summit. We were paid by a grand view of the country, city, harbor and ocean. We inscribed our names upon a rock beside those of adventurers who had preceeded us and started down rattling the loose rock before and frightening numerous huge black lizards, the only permanent inhabitants. When we reached the bottom of the mountain a hard wind was blowing and a tremendous surf breaking on the rocks. It was with trouble and danger we were taken into the boats that came from the ship for us.

Here the original Vermont party took passage in another vessel, while we on the sixth day hove anchor and sailed away on the last long stretch that would land us at our wished for haven, but providence or the fates had otherwise ordained, as will appear.

After leaving Mazatlan our quarters and fare on the *Mary Frances* almost intollerable. There the captain, contrary to our protest, took as passengers about forty more dirty, black greasers, male and female, crowding the steerage so close that the air between decks was horrible. We could not endure it and were driven to living and sleeping on the upper deck tops, boats or wherever we could get away from the filthy creatures. The food furnished us steerage passengers was damaged jerkie, wormy, musty hard bread, weevily rice and tea with molasses for sweetening, all cooked in the aforementioned whalers' try kettles. There were some pigs aboard for cabin use. Each night the cooks would scald a pig in one of the kettles, then bail it out and break with hammers over the side of the kettle a lot of jerkie and ship biscuit, to which was added a sack of rice, and the mess was boiled through the night for our next day's grub. As a fact, we often found hogs hairs in the lobscouse. We did not mind these things so much until after a few days our private supplies were gone.

Right here I must tell of the first time I met a whale. One night about 12 o'clock when our ship was somewhere off the Gulf of California, when not able longer to stand the heat and smell of the steerage, I went on deck. It was a glorious moonlight night, not a breath of air, the sea was smooth as glass, the moonlight glanced on the water like a sheen of silver. I climbed up on the counter and sat with my feet hanging over the ship's side, arms laced in the rigging, all alone. My thoughts far away to that distant Iowa home. All was quiet on the ship and I was almost in a dream when suddenly right before my eyes and not fifty feet from where I was sitting there arose a huge and monstrous form, thirty-forty and as it seemed to me then a hundred feet in height. I was startled and frightened, but as he turned to dive I knew it was a whale. In a few moments the sea around was full of whales, plunging and diving. The wonder was where they all came from so quietly. The ship rocked from the waves they raised by their gambolling, and the officers expressed fear that they might collide with us. They fired several times a small gun from the forecastle, but the whales did not scare. They stayed around several hours.

On the tenth day at sea it was discovered that by the neglect of the drunken mate we were already short of water and so perforce bore up for Cape San Lucas, entering the harbor or rather roadstead of San Jose the 6th of April. Here, induced by reports of the practicability of the route by land, some eight or ten of us agreed to leave the old floating coffin and take our chance ashore and up the peninsula by land, but before the vessel sailed all but four, of which I was one, backed out and tried to frighten us—but we were bound to go through or die trying. Indeed, we believed our chances quite as safe and good ashore as on a rotten ship.

From what we had read or could learn and from a chart we had, on which was laid down numerous towns and missions, we thought it would be but a pleasant horseback canter of some thirty or forty days to San Francisco, and that over a Champaign country dotted with ranches and missions and covered with herds of innumerable cattle and horses. We would make money by taking horses and mules through to the mines and then there was a charm in the wild novelty of the thing that impeled us to dare do what others feared.

It was not without a feeling of loneliness we bade good-bye to our companions and gazed after the old barque until she disappeared around the headland, leaving us on our own resources to prosecute a journey through an almost unknown wilderness for 1,000 or more miles to San Diego, the first place of which we had any certain knowledge, could expect to see a countryman or obtain any relief.

Had we really known what was before us, the undertaking might well have been called foolhardy. Before commencing an account of the journey let me give a more particular description of my companions and their characters:

First and foremost, William F. Nye, a true blue, about 25 years of age, a graduate of Harvard College and Law School, admitted to the New York bar, of brilliant talents, an only son of wealthy parents. Yet to gratify his love of adventure had already made a voyage to China before the mast. A generous and self-denying friend, but an inveterate enemy; brave as a lion, yet gentle as a woman. Dear Nye! How can I do you justice? When I think of all you and I have gone through together, how you and I stuck to one another in gloom as in sunshine, I feel in my heart that there is something behind that little brown visage of yours, a congenial sparkle in the light of those black eyes, that will endear our memories to each other so long as we may live.

Next in order of my estimation comes Israel Miller, the lieutenant, or as we generally said, "Old Miller." He was 28 years of age, medium size, but muscular and powerful. Served with distinction on Scott's line during the Mexican War; was one of the first to mount the walls of Chapultepec. For this gallantry his regiment presented him an elegant sword. From some cause, probably a family trouble to which he once casually alluded, he was given to spells of dejection, almost amounting to sulkiness. These humors annoyed us until we became accustomed to this. He was a good man and in any difficulty always a trump card.

As for the third member of our party, I will stay my pen. He is dead now, let him rest. He taught us how a pleasant countenance and fascinating manner might conceal the most black hearted treachery. Twice did that villain get up in the night while he thought we slept and steal the last drop of water from our canteens—water which in extremity we had equally divided. Yet we spared him. He was brave and energetic, and that is all I can record to his credit.

Thus was our band composed of four stalwart young men, all of good nerve and iron constitution.

San Jose is a village of about 500 inhabitants, situated on the narrow flat formed by the mouth of a small stream, and facing the ocean to the south. It has not much of a harbor. While we were there it was calm weather, but the combing waves were always rolling in upon the sand beach 8 or 10 feet high, and it required skill and practice to make a safe landing or launch. One boatload from our ship was capsized and rolled over and over.

A high, steep and barren mountain overhangs the town on the north. On each side of the stream as high as water can be led for irrigation are growing oranges, lemons, bananas, plantains, sugar cane and other tropical plants. The people here make sugar in small brown cakes and eat it freely. They call it "panoche." During the war the town was occupied by a detachment from Stevenson's regiment. Two field guns left by them were standing in the court yard of the old mission. The place appears to be going to decay.

We were treated well by the people. We got into a row with a Mexican army captain about a mule we were both trying to buy. He first threatened with his pistols, but as we did not scare he appealed the case to the alcalde, who, to our surprise, gave the mule to us. The captain was bound on the same route and, when he found us proof against both bravado and law, was very willing to be friendly. After two days' bargaining we picked up, in addition to our pack mule, four spare, bony horses, quite different animals from the sleek *cavallos* we expected to find.

About 12 M., April 10th, we got off. We hired an "ombre" to teach the mysteries of packing a mule and to show us one league on the road to Todos Santos, at which place the old guide said there were many good "bestias" for sale cheap. So we punched up old Joe, as we had christened the venerable animal that carried our scanty budgets, bade good-bye to the guide, spurred a trot out of our hacks and pushed along in good spirits.

From this place I kept an imperfect journal, which I shall copy verbatim, adding as memory serves such remembrances as may be interesting to those for whom these things are recorded. I have confidence in their respect and affection or would not risk their thinking my narrations to be traveller's tales. Let me assure them I write but of facts. "quam vidi, et & c."

April 10th, left San Jose at 11 a.m. Country wild and rugged. Horses sure-footed. Camped at sundown in the mountains by a pretty stream. Scenery wild and romantic. I am thinking of someone far away who will not forget me, we are in good spirits. This undertaking may be unwise but it has the charm of novelty. Eight leagues. God prosper us.

I well remember that first camp in a little mountain valley under a large live oak tree. I was the only one who understood camp life, and was by acclamation installed chief cook. I got up a supper of jerkie fried on the coals and coffee, which the boys pronounced first rate. We all ate with perfect gusto. Nye remarked, "How I pity those poor fellows at sea." Even old Miller got up a grim smile. We all joined in singing "Old Virginia" and "I'm Bound for California" until the rocks rang again; then rolled up in our blankets quite happy.

April 11th—Another day among the mountains. Path difficult, country wild and picturesque, well watered. Horned frogs and scorpions plenty. Camped by a stream. Ten leagues. (We were under the impression here that we should soon get out of the mountains into a beautiful, level champaigne country, abounding in horses, cattle, etc., little thinking that we were leaving behind the only tolerable region between Cape San Lucas and San Diego.)

April 12th—Country improving. Five leagues by the sea shore. Todos Santos at 4 o'clock p.m. An oasis. People intelligent and pleasant. Had much curiosity at meeting Americanos, and to know where we were going. A large mission building, mostly in ruins, a relic of the Jesuits. Twelve leagues. (As we rode down from the mountains the wind was blowing fresh off the sea and the breakers coming in ten feet high. We galloped along the hard, smooth beach in great glee. The shore was strewn with quantities of rare and most beautiful shells. We gathered a great many, but did not carry them many days. We saw here for the first time heaped in reefs by the waves a plant or animal, which afterwards we found all along the coast. It was a hollow tube from one to four inches in diameter and 100 or more feet in length, with near one end an oval cylinder of perhaps the size of a half barrel. The substance was like dark rubber and smelled like flesh. Todos Santos was the prettiest and most fruitful place we saw in "Abajo."—Lower California is so called in distinction from the country above San Diego, which is always spoken of as the "Alta". There were perhaps 1000 acres in a high state of cultivation, irrigated by a small river of sweet water which was diverted into hundreds of tiny channels, all finally sinking in the sand near the sea shore. About where the water sank and on each side of the cultivated land were growing many tall Drascenia palms and dense brakes of common cane. This was the most flourishing of the establishments of the Jesuits on the peninsula, one of the few producing a surplus of provisions, which accounts for it still being occupied. The mission has been suppressed seventy years, and was not transferred to the Franciscans as many other of the missions were. We purchased here one good horse and a mule, the last the most beautiful animal of the kind I have ever seen. She cost us fifty dollars, an immense price when fine mules are sold for twenty. We bought her from the padre. She was his saddle mule. We prized the little beauty, "Jule" as we called her, highly.)

April 13th—Left Todos Santos at 12 o'clock M. Trail along the seaside. I shot three geese and a large, strange bird. Lost our way among the sand hills and camped after dark without water or grass. (We thought that night it was pretty hard times). After a fruitless search for water, or some indication of the lost trail, darkness compelled us to throw down on a sandy plain, literally covered with thorny cactus. Unable to eat from thirst we turned in supperless. This taught us that water might be an uncertain commodity and we did not forget the lesson.

April 14th — A hard day for man and beast. Started early. Rode without food or drink until 2 p.m. Found a pond of brackish water. Horrid stuff! The horses would not drink it. We made some coffee, but it was no go. Pushed on until dark to a little deserted brush shanty where we found a small pool of repulsive, bitter water. This day we have suffered much (we did not know what suffering was yet). The road good along the sea. This is a desert in reality. About 25 leagues from Todos Santos. Early in the day we found growing by a salt pond several clumps of tomato plants bearing fruit the size of peas. They tasted grateful to our parched mouths. We thought they must be indigenous. That afternoon old Joe made an estampede. It was a way he had when the trail or anything else did not suit him. Nye chased him around among the cactus for an hour perfectly furious at the old villian. Despite our troubles we could not help laughing at the old rascal's maneuvers and dodges. Our camp was a sorry place. Fare dry jerked beef and hard bread solo.

April 15th, Sunday — Detained two hours hunting for Nye's horse. Road much as yesterday. A barren plain along the coast, broken by ravines, destitute of water, no vegetation but cactus. A mountain range in the distance to the east. Camped early near another deserted brush ranch. Have dug a well and found tolerable water. Enough for ourselves and the poor animals. The Pacific is roaring within a few rods. We have gathered drift wood on the beach and built a big fire on the lee side of a high rock. Ten leagues today. What a life! "Home, Sweet Home," how my thoughts travel back! and how little do you all know what I am enduring. Now for my blanket on the ground. (These ranches I mentioned were brush huts, the temporary shelter of herdsmen, when from rains there might happen to be feed for stock, and were the only signs of habitation). Our camp was a romantic place, a small, rocky promontory on which the sea dashed with fury, roaring and rumbling in the caverns worn in the rocks by the beating waves. Many rugged crags stood breasting the surge out from the shore. In the night I was awakened by the most hideous screaming and howling imaginable. I thought we were beset by a legion of wild beasts and in haste seized my gun and woke Nye. He, an old sailor, at once recognized the voices of sea lions, in what so alarmed me. They were all around the camp attracted by the fire. Though reassured, I slept no more that night.

April 16th—I was aroused this morning by the cry, "come, boys, four o'clock." We soon saddled up and were off. The trail left the coast and took off among the sand hills. About noon a horse gave out from hunger and thirst. We left him to perish. Late at night we found water, much to our joy. There is no grass, but we were obliged to stop. The poor animals are failing fast, provisions almost gone and San Luis the only place we know of an indefinite distance ahead. Have seen no one since we left Todos Santos. A crisis in our affairs seems near at hand, but "never say die" is our watchword. The boys are singing "Oh, Susanna, Don't You Cry for Me." I must join. We have made a rule to never turn in without singing a cheerful song.

April 17th—This morning old Joe had vamoosed and left us in a fix. After several hours' fruitless search we packed our jaded horses and prepared for a gloomy march on foot. Just them B came in from the hunt and with him an Indian, who told us of an inhabited ranch a few miles in the interior and, guided by him, we repaired there at once, and here we are trying to recruit ourselves and animals and buy some more horses. Indulging the while in plenty of food and water. We have found here a gentlemanly Portugese, the son-in-law of the proprietor. He speaks English. (From what they told us here, our expedition came near being brought to a termination. The trail we intended taking would have led through a sandy desert without grass or water seventy miles to Magdalena Bay, where we would have found neither, nor any within a hundred miles further on. Our only escape would have been to come directly back and this we would not have done even if we could. The trail was one used by the natives when at certain seasons they went down to the bay to trade with whalers, and then they packed water with them. So in all probability old Joe saved us there. A vaquero brought him in that evening.)

April 18th—Laid by all day at the rancho, buying horses and making provision for continuing our journey. People very kind. The Portuguese intelligent. He has a fine vineyard and fruit trees in a valley back in the mountains. My new horse is a beauty, but wild like these Californians themselves. Much interested by their wonderful performance with the lasso. This seems a good specimen of a California ranch. The old proprietor is as one of the ancient Patriarchs. They are a better people than the Mexicans. Now to my blanket. They have spread ox hides on the ground for us to lie on, quite a mark of civility towards us. This place is called the Rancho Colorado, from the river of that name, on the bank of which it is situated. The house is a long, low rambling concern built of canes and brush interwoven. The roof of weeds and flags. One half of one side open, a ground floor. In the corner of one room is a clay furnace for cooking. The river is dry now, except a deep pond of several acres which is the water supply for the establishment. Under a shed, suspended to posts, are two large vessels of porous earthenware which are kept filled with water for drinking and in which the water becomes very cool. (The Portugese told us that years sometimes passed without the river flowing, but occasionally it was furious, as was apparent from the immense channel and marks of destruction. Such is the character of most of the streams in the Abajo. At the time we passed there had been scarcely any rain for five years. The people live almost entirely upon beef cooked every way except any mode we were accustomed to, but they never fail to add chili pepper enough to bring tears from the eyes of a dried codfish. We bought a steer and had the peons dress and jerk the meat for us. They roasted the head, hair, bones and all with hot stones in a hole in the ground. They politely invited us to share. We were not fastidious and laid hold. It was perfectly delicious. They were much interested in our revolvers. Had never before seen such a weapon; but what they most coveted was tobacco. Our stock of that was low, and Nye and I were smokers. Yet we divided with them. Afterwards we smoked willow bark ourselves. The old proprietor was once a leading politician in Mexico. Was exiled to this place by the Emperor Iturbide. He had here an immense tract of semi-desert land on which ranged several thousand cattle and horses, his sole wealth. We learned from Francisco that the journey before us was a serious affair. He gave us much advice that was of timely benefit. He told us of a party who, from lack of precaution, had not long before perished on the same route. Under his supervision there was made for us a number of leather water bottles, which they all charged us to fill at every opportunity. They told us to throw away our Mexican bridles with their huge steel bits and ride our horses with hackamores, or head halters, and also provided us a good stock of dried beef and pinole, which is wheat ground by hand on a tortillia stone.)

April 19th — Packed up this morning at 10 o'clock and with regret bade adieu to our good friends at the rancho. Their kindness we felt to be in such contrast to this horrid country. Especially you, Francisco Betanca, I grieve to think that in all probability I shall see you no more forever. We made them all a gift of some kind from our scanty stock. I gave Francisco my red silk scarf which he had admired. They sent a man this far to guide us on the right way to San Luis. The path is rugged over shelving rocks, hills and dry river beds. Five fresh horses make our cavalcade imposing and carry us along finely. We camped at 6 p.m. on the bank of the Rio Passeo with wood, water and plenty of grass. Fourteen leagues. (The grass was always dry like hay. Horses do well on such feed. The trouble was its scarcity. To one who has never seen such a region it is hard to describe the awful sterility of the country we passed over for many days thereafter.)

April 20th — Broke camp at 6 o'clock. Over many stones reached San Luis at 12 m. Now this was one of the places laid down on our chart, and from what they told us at the Rancho Colorado, and I am sure they told us all they knew, we expected to find at least a small village, but it is only an old deserted Jesuit mission in ruins. It stands solitary in the midst of desolation. Searching around we found an old decrepit Indian who lived somewhere in the building. He showed us some paintings of the Madonna and the Saints in good preservation. The mission is a large stone building and has been a fine specimen of Spanish architecture. We asked the old fellow for eggs, bread, tortillias or anything to eat, but all we could get out of him was, "Nada, nada! por comair!" (nothing, nothing! to eat!"). However, after some persuasion he produced some food. Camp eight leagues from San Luis. No water tonight but our canteens, and no certainty when we shall have. There is nothing so fearful to us in this parched desert as that we may not find water. (The old Indian at the mission was not disposed to sell us anything, nor would he tell us anything about the trail or the country. As we had expected we found this disposition manifested frequently by this people, and more often threats were more effective with them than persuasion.)

April 21st—Started early. Have all day been wandering among rocks and over mountains. For many leagues have had no trail. We are lost. How will we get out of this scrape? Fortunately we have found water and grass. We are bewildered but not discouraged.

April 22nd—Under way at 6. Found the trail. What a cursed country! Rocks, thorns and this horrid cactus! The devil's own plant. Old Joe, confound him, got up several estampedes. Plenty of water, but little grass. Nye shot a huge rattlesnake. We are hard up but full of spirit. My only pair of breeches in rags, used up by the thorns. Well, my skin is sound yet. (Almost the only vegetation was cactus of every size, shape and form. It frequently formed a barrier through which we were obliged to force our horses, the long, sharp points piercing us and them. The ground everywhere was literally covered with thorny plants. Indeed, the region seemed to have been gotten up in a spirit of malediction.)

April 23rd—Another day of toil and vexation. Had a two-hour hunt for a horse this morning. Road rugged, one tremendous steep mountain side. Stones upon stones. These stones in the trail look like pieces of broken blackjunk bottles. They are obsidian and cut like knives. The poor unshod horses leave blood at every track. Provisions are failing. Have not seen a human being this side of San Luis. Ten leagues. (In places there was a broad, almost level surface, apparently lava flow. Fields of this shivered shattered obsidian. Off the trail on either side were impassable cracks and fissures.)

April 24th—Started at 9. Found a small ranch where we got a few provisions. Lost the road and after wandering up and down and over the most horrible mountain I ever saw, here we are at 10 at night stuck in a deep ravine, on a bed of rocks, without grass or water. I am keeping up a fire of dry cactus, and by the light the boys are trying to level a spot where we can sleep without breaking our necks. I never conceived a road could be so bad, but our horses seem to climb like cats. (That was a miserable night. I remember how we sang many cheerful songs to keep up courage. How old Nye would say, "Come, brace up, boys. Now, one more song." We learned that day that we had straggled from the coast trail which we should have kept into the "Camino Arrieva" or mountain road.)

April 25th — All day the trail has led through the bed of a dry river. Some places good, at others difficult. In an opening of the ravine we were surprised to come upon a large, fine, cut-stone building, a mass of arches, towers and pinnacles. The tile roofs and stone walls were in good preservation. The grounds around had been terraced with walls, and no doubt were once productive, but now the walls which confined the earth are broken down, and where once were blooming gardens, is now a barren waste. Nothing remains but the desolate edifice, a few stunted date trees and some stumps of vines, to tell of the great labors and weary self-denial of the good old fathers and of the mission of San Gabriel. My San Jose horse gave out. Left him by the road. Met a man and gave him the horse to guide us to Comondu. Very poor feed for the horses tonight. We have a feast of fresh beef and soup. Camp in a narrow valley. High mountains around. (In the afternoon we came to a place where some natives — Indians — were roasting mescal roots. The process is by heating rocks in a hole and then covering the rocks and roots with earth for a day or more. The mescal is a plant much like the agave. They had a little beef and rather unwillingly sold us some. The costume of these "hombres" was so simple and natural as would be best described by saying nothing.)

April 26th — All day among the rocks and mountains. Little to be noticed, always excepting the cursed cactus, which is everywhere, and of every shape. Passed two huts, where we got some milk and a little bitter wine. I forgot my gun and sent the guide back for it. The boys said I would never see gun or guide again, but he disappointed them. Bad water, poor grass. Horses footsore. Ten leagues.

April 27th — All day the so-called road wound over a table mountain. the most barren region imaginable. The earth, or rather the rocks, have been convulsed in a singular manner, and piled fantastically one on another. It could not be more rugged. Over such a country we picked a difficult way, depressed by the suffering of the poor horses and the utter desolation around us. Unexpectedly we came to the margin of a great chasm. Someone said, "See, there is Comondu." Looking down, there lay some 2000 feet below us a perfect picture. A beautiful little valley, green as an emerald, while the sunlightd glancing from water fairly made the very horses laugh. Impulsively we scrambled down the barranca side at a breakneck pace, and soon arrived, to the satisfaction of man and beast. We were tired out, but here we now are enjoying plenty of good food and sweet water, and our famished horses are revelling in green grass up to their knees. This is another station of the good padres. Judging by the work they did, there must have been many more people in the country in their time than now. A place could not be more secluded than this, yet the people appear happy. They are quite civilized and a large proportion are part-blood Castilian. The valley is about two miles long and two or three hundred yards wide. Plenty of running water which they say never fails. The principal productions are corn, grass, sugar cane, oranges, olives, figs, bananas, pomegranates, melons and grapes. From the latter they make an astringent wine, like a bad port. Here we will lay in supplies of food and so forth for the next objective point, San Ignacio. We must be coming within the gold mining influence, things are getting dear. They have heard here of the "Auro," and some have even already gone from this valley of content to search for it in the alta.

April 28th—Resting at Comondu. In the morning repaired my tattered clothing. In the afternoon rode up the valley and went through the mission building. It is a fine, large stone structure in good condition. In the belfry is suspended a chime of four large Spanish bells. One bore a cast inscription, "Valladolid 1643." Bought a fine horse for $25. Saw many vines and fruit trees. The valley is all closely intersected with small irrigating canals and all cultivated. We feasted on strawberries. Have hired a guide and will start in the morning. Now to my blankets and saddle pillow.

April 29th—Slept well and long and dreamed of home. Purchased a mule and at 5 p.m. packed up and with regret bade adieu to Comondu, the valley of the vine and fig tree. Rode about a league down the canyon and camped under trees by the brookside. Horses feasting on sweet clover. Like my new horse very much. The animals are improved by rest and food. Fine moonlight. 10 o'clock, turn in.

April 30th—Started at six. Valley soon opened out into the coast desert and the brook disappeared in the sand. Good-bye, sweet clover! Turned to the right over low sand hills and into the camino abajo. Killed a large rattlesnake in the trail. Once more on the Pacific coast. This guide is an old fool. "No saccate ake" (no grass here). Late march. Camp at 8. Ten leagues. (We thought the guide knew nothing of the country because he found no grass, afterward we knew we had wronged the old fellow, for there was no grass to be found, only burrs and thorns.)

May 1st—May Day. What are they doing at home? God grant all are well. Started very early. Rio Purissma and a little ranch. Brackish water. Rio San Gregorio, very salty. Hills of loose, drifted sand. Joe estampedes. Camp near the sea. Fourteen leagues. No grass. My pipe is out. Good night. (Miller and the mule had a long race that day over the sand hills and through the cactus. I could have pardoned the lieutenant had he killed him as he vowed he would. Our camp was in a singular place, on a flat behind a bank of sand thrown up by the sea, perhaps 100 feet high and extending each way as far as could be seen. We climbed up the steep land side to the top of the ridge and were surprised to find that the land where we camped was many feet lower than the ocean. It may have been high tide. The sand at our camp was full of scorpions. We always scraped a place to sleep for fear of scorpions, tarantulas or centipedes, but that night I remember they were so plenty we gathered a quantity of dry cactus and burned off a sleeping place.)

May 2nd—Sand hills. Gallop along the smooth beach. Many beautiful shells. Wish I could carry some with me. Seals and sea lions lying out on the rocks. Small spring of fresh water. Leave the seaside. Rocky hills. Many stones. Camp late in a little valley. No pasture. Moonlight 11 o'clock. Thirteen leagues.

May 3rd—Country rolling. Barren as usual. San Jose de Gracias vines, figs, oranges and bananas. As usual "no nar nada por comair," that is, we have nothing to eat. Short stay. Steep mountain climb by a stony trail. Late march. All in an ill humor. Camp at 10 p.m. on a bleak mountain top without grass or water. Fasten horses and mules to cactus stumps. It is cold. Eighteen leagues. Twelve o'clock.

May 4th—Morning cold. Stones! Stones! Stones! Up and down steep hills and deep barrancas. Miserable country. Not a blade of dry grass all day. At noon came to El Patricio, an adobe mission in ruins. An Indian family in a corner room of the old building. Water and palm trees, "a diamond in the desert." Got some food for ourselves and cane leaves for the horses. Camp in a valley all rocks. No grass again. Slim supper, one long-treasured, small bologna sausage for five men. Twelve leagues.

May 5th—Country all the same. About noon found off the trail a small spring of sweet water, with cane growing around, on which we fed our starving animals. At 6 p.m. came to a hut in a pretty little valley. It was inhabited by an American, a native of Connecticut. He had lived here alone many years. He said he came to this coast with Commodore Porter on the U.S. Ship *Essex* in 1813. He could scarcely speak English. Left our guide here. Pushing on made San Ignacio at 10 p.m. Much jaded. The mission building looks splendid by moonlight.

May 6th—This mission of San Ignacio is the largest and best preserved of these old establishments we have seen. We spent much of the day rambling through the building. The interiors of the rooms are well finished with plaster, frescoes, carved woodwork and paintings. Much of the color on the walls is yet fresh and bright, and it seems as if the padres had just left. In the refractory were stone tables and stone benches and on the plastered wall was plain to be seen the mark of greasy heads made many years ago. There are some good framed pictures of the Saviour and Saints, and one large historical painting of the naval battle of Lepanto, the remarkable feature of which is the Heavenly Father above in the clouds directing a host of angels who are hurling fiery darts upon the poor Turks. Don Juan of Austria is about four times the ordinary stature and is swinging a flaming sword. How interesting are these relics! It seems almost like what is told of Tadmor and Petrea. So massive and beautiful, yet deserted in a wilderness. I remember reading of the Padres "Ugart" and "Salva Tierra," who led the way and gave their lives to this great and humane endeavor of the Jesuits to Christianize and ameliorate the condition of the miserable savages in this inhospitable region. About 100 half-civilized Indians live around in mud huts covered with cane leaves. They are kept together by a superstitious reverance for the old place, which they keep clean. They dare not touch to injure or take away anything. Even the silver censer and other vessels of silver remain on the altar. A priest comes once a year to marry and baptize them and to say mass for the dead. When the old Indian who guided us through the building pointed out San Christo (Christ), San Paulo, San Ignacio and other saints, I asked him, "Which of these is the biggest man?" He seemed surprised at my ignorance and answered quickly, "San Ignacio, senor. He is the greatest of all." "What kind of a man was San Christo?" "Oh, muy bueno hombre, no mucho grande" (a very good man, but not very big). The boys have gone to a fandango. I am alone by the campfire, thinking of home and the friends there, who I am sure are thinking of me, a weary wanderer. A long road is yet before us. Horses weak, money scarce, clothes in rags and bare-footed save slips of rawhide, but we are not discouraged. Tomorrow's sun must see us many miles hence. (Here we had to choose between two routes, the Camino Abajo by the ocean coast over sandy plains, with neither grass nor water for nine days, except what we could pack. This route would in ten days take us to Rosario, a point we must make, but we knew that in the weak condition of our animals we would never get through, so we have determined to attempt, without a guide, a trail over the mountains to the gulf and thence back to the coast. This we were told was a twenty days' journey, but we would find water and grass occassionally).

May 10th — All but myself have turned in. I am alone by the fire tending a pot of soup for breakfast, and will try to bring up my neglected journal. God knows there has been enough lately to prevent my writing. We were detained in San Ignacio the sixth purchasing a horse. Next morning our best mule, a valuable and beautiful creature, was missing. These people had tried to buy or trade us other mules for her. Failing that the cutthroat villains had stolen her and hidden her away in the mountains, where we could not find her. They took advantage of our necessity to ask an exorbitant price for any other mule, far more than we could afford to pay. Our remaining animals had not strength to pack our scanty baggage, provisions and the water which we must carry, so we were stuck fast. All we could get to replace our pretty Jule was a miserable old horse. We went to the Indian alcalde. He only laughed at us. The day before he could talk Spanish fast enough. Now all we could get out of him was "no intende"—don't understand. We were sure that he was the very thief. We could not bear to give up the only animal we could depend on. It seemed like risking our lives to go on without having her to pack water. In our anger we almost cried. We left the place the evening of the seventh and for three days have been getting along bad enough; our animals have suffered much. This afternoon we found this spring of water and grass just in time to save their lives and our own. Two horses lost in one day from thirst. We fear they will all go soon. We have thrown away all baggage not indispensible. We are at least twenty days from San Diego and will probably make a barefoot march through this horrid, mountainous desert. The only water we found from San Ignacio here was in a deep rock cavern, and that bitter. We are in a difficult position, but must go on. I never before found myself in quite so tight a place. We are all good game yet and whistle and sing when we can.

I will now record a transaction omitted from my journal because I had not yet seen and suffered quite enough to be satisfied that "necessity knew no law":

We did not know the full value of our good mule until at last we started without her. After beating along the miserable old substitute about three miles we halted and, after consultation, agreed that while one kept camp the others should go back and make one more attempt to recover Jule. That failing, we would at all hazard seize the best mule we could find. So leaving B, three of us put our pistols in order and mounting the best horses returned to the village. Our search and demands were of no avail; though we threatened to burn the whole place unless they produced her, so we openly took possession of the alcalde's best mule and led it off to camp. We then packed it and started on; traveling all night to elude pursuit. Making a short halt in the morning, we pushed on over a dreadful road. About the middle of the afternoon while winding through a narrow chasm, we found ourselves surrounded by an overpowering band of black rascals, armed with escopets. We kept those on the trail before and behind at a distance with pointed guns, but on each side above they were prepared to roll rocks upon us. They had us in a trap. It was evident they could finally kill us in such a place. We were out of water and so, preferring discretion to useless valor, we turned the mule loose; after which they did not molest us. It was well for them for we had forty shots in hand and were desperate.

For the next two days our suffering was very great. It was by a last struggle we reached this water spring. Before leaving there we determined to obtain what we must have to live peaceably if we could, but forcibly if we must, and that we had as well die one way as another. In that spirit we prosecuted the rest of our journey to San Diego.

With some reluctance I must tell how near our expedition came to a tragic close. The facts are like a horrid dream. On the ninth the trail was over a dry desert, where tracks left but a dimple in the hot sand. Neither water or grass all the day. At night we threw down on the plain, tied the animals to cactus, we divided and drank our last few swallows of bitter water and laid down. We could not eat, could not sleep from thirst. We started early in the morning. The sun came up as a great ball of fire. To the east was a range of hills. There was the only chance for water. We traveled for them. About noon two horses laid down and died. We came to a dry canyon. The heat was intense. Our tongues were so swollen we could scarcely speak. Presently the canyon grew narrow. A high rock threw a few feet of shade on the burning sand. All men and animals crowded into this shade, but this would not do. B. and I drove out the animals. Nye and Miller laid down by the rock and would not come. There was no time to lose; it was simply find water soon or die. We left them. We had not gone a mile up the canyon before a jackass, one we had bought from the Rancho Colorado, pricked up his ears, gave a loud bray and started on a run square off up the steep side of the canyon. All the other animals followed pell-mell up the hillside, over the ridge and out of sight in a cloud of dust. B. and I climbed slowly after them to the top and there looking down we saw a little green valley, a water brook and the mules and horses standing in the water and drinking. We got there quickly and drank our fill. Then we filled two leather bottles with water and I hurried back to the rock. Nye and Miller were both asleep in a stupor. I poured water in their mouths and with effort aroused them. That time the instinct or sense of a jackass saved us — but for the jackass we never would have found that water.

May 12th, Sunday — At 3 p.m. yesterday we left the camp by the stream, and left with regret. We had suffered so much from want of water we did not like to go away from this sweet spring. The horses' feet were so sore we could scarcely force them over the stones, and were compelled to walk. For several hours we wound up a steep mountain several thousand feet, the gulf, islands and what we supposed to be the opposite coast in full view. Before us rose peak upon peak of bare, burnt rocks. The scene altogether barren and forbidding. One might well think there was a curse resting upon this region; this perfection of eternal desolation. In the whole expanse not a living thing save the never failing cactus, which itself is a curse in many forms. The ascent was difficult and the descent equally painful, one barranca succeeding another. Night found us in a deep, dark gorge, not a star visible. Thirsty and without water we laid down on the rocks supperless. When we left the spring we filled Nye's rubber pillow in addition to the leather water bottles, but somehow it was all gone. Water! Water!! What will one not give for it under such circumstances. We broke up this morning before day, and following down the ravine reached this little mission of Santa Gertrude. We asked to buy food, but as usual, "no hai nada," but we compelled them to sell us some beans and barley bread. What once was the mission garden is now a marshy canebrake. We pulled down the wall and turned in our horses. Poor progress, only 36 leagues in five days. At this rate we will be all summer reaching San Francisco. For the next three days there is in places an herb poisonous to animals. To guard against it we take a guide to San Borzia. This morning we left a horse to die. In the old mission are a number of Catholic paintings and some gold or gilded ornaments. Our clothes are much dilapidated. Could our friends see us they would think we suffered intollerably, while in fact we are completely hardened and try to think of nothing but getting out of this predicament. Today I observed twelve species of cactus — confound them all. Noticed yesterday on the mountain two new and singular varieties, one like a large, round bottom basket inverted and thick-set with spikes six inches long, but bearing magnificent crimson flowers.

There were two Indian families here. They had several animals, one a jackass, a much hardier creature than a horse or mule. We wanted him to pack water and offered them treble his value, but they would not sell him. So we paid them a big price and, to use Nye's language, "annexed" him, and at first called him Texas, but finally "Paul," after a picture in the mission, and then the jack who found the water already was christened "Peter."

May 18th—On Monday at 3 a.m. we left Santa Gertrude and proceeded down the Pacific slope over rock and stone. About 10 a.m. the trail turned and again began to ascend the dividing ridge. We noticed that the blue volcanic trap rock and black obsidian had changed to granite and stratified gneiss. The first time we had met with primitive rock. Reached the summit at noon. We had made our guide a liberal advance payment, and here, where we would first need him, he gave us the slip. So we descended alone into what to our fears was as a valley of death. Our apprehensions were kept alive by frequently seeing skeletons of horses. After four days struggling through the mountains and enduring hunger and thirst we arrived at this place. San Francisco Borghia, entirely out of provisions and nearly famished. Last night we pounded an old piece of rawhide and boiled it for soup. This is a poor place to recruit. There is but one family of five Indians. They are living on mescal root. We cannot eat it. It is for us like castor oil. All we can get from them to eat is green peas and beans. They have a small patch of barley not quite ripe. The women are drying the plucked heads in earthen olios over a fire, shelling and pounding the grain, to prepare us a small stock of pinole for the road. There are some wild rabbits about the ruins. Nye and B. are trying to shoot them. I think we can keep soul and body together until we reach Rosario, eleven days hence, where they say there is meat. We have taken possession of a room in the massive old ruin, our fire is built on the paved floor of pieces of broken doors and window shutters. These doors and shutters are curious. They are about four inches thick and all made of small pieces of very hard wood ingeniously dovetailed together.

We wonder where the padres got this wood and how and by whom all this work was done. There is something very impressive about these solid old buildings. We keep a pot of peas constantly boiling, trying to fill ourselves, but they give little strength without salt or fat. We are altered in feeling as in appearance, but yet try to keep up our spirits. Forty-six leagues from Santa Gertrude.

May 26th—My journal is sadly neglected. It gives me no pleasure. It is only a monotonous record of suffering and disaster. We made San Fernando this morning in eight days. Sixty-two leagues from San Borghia. Soon after we left San Borghia we were overtaken by our San Jose captain, an old Rosario man with a train and another party of Mexicans, all bound for the "Alta." The two latter parties had crossed the gulf from Guymas to Lorretto. They were all better equipped and left us. The road and country have been notably execrable, even for this horrid land. Hot, sandy plains, stony mountains, scarcity of water and food. Barefooted men and sore-footed horses make up a catalogue of trouble. One mule made a dead set—would go no further. We shot her to save a lingering death. Our fare has been a small measured daily portion of barley pinole and a little tallow bought by much coaxing from the Rosario man; also an eagle which I was fortunate to shoot. We made soup of him. He was too tough to eat. Three nights ago, after crossing the worst mountain of the whole route, we camped by the ruins of the mission of Santa Maria, in view of and near the gulf. We could not imagine why the padres ever built a house in such a place. So barren that there was no sign for many miles on either side of any life and, save the weak, little spring, there could have been no inducement. It showed strongly the value of water in such a thirsty land. Now we are once more on the Pacific slope. We have crossed the dividing ridge six times from San Ignacio, and hope to not see the gulf again. Several of the horses were just able to reach this place. Two days more to Rosario, where we hope to and must procure some fresh animals, or go afoot. As it is we walk nearly all the way, and could get along faster without the horses, but we can't carry water and we have no shoes. This old ruin is a miserable place. Three or four root-eating Indians live in a corner of the house, where they have patched the fallen roof with cane leaves. They have preserved superstitiously some old defaced images and pictures. In this time of trouble I think often of home and friends far away. Perhaps it would have been better for me had I not left them. I am glad they know nothing of this situation. Our endurance is not near at an end. Our courage rises against difficulties. We have more confidence in the future, knowing what we have already overcome. San Francisco is our watchword and out of this darkness the Alta still looms up like a star of hope. (The last two entries need no supplement. They are enough alone without comment but I must here say that in the worst times our scanty store of food and water was always divided impartially and that we constantly strove to help and encourage each other. Nye was a hero, in every straight he acted with noble courage and self-denial.)

From here there is an interim in my notes which I will fill from recollection. Three days more through a desert, with little to live on but faith, brought us to Rosario. On the road we shot two worn-out horses to save them from starvation. Our cavalcade that entered the village was rather sorry. For weeks our fare had been slim and this, in addition to walking over sharp flints with no protection to our feet but slips of rawhide, had reduced our strength exceedingly. So it was with satisfaction we saw hanging to a tree parts of a newly slaughtered beef. We soon invested a large part of our capital in a huge piece and, camping at the first convenient spot, commenced broiling and eating until we were gorged. As a consequence, in an hour's time, every one of us was very sick. We remained three days, resting and recruiting with plenty of food, water and grass. Here we again met with trees, live oak and sycamore. We exchanged several worn-out horses and some blankets for a good horse and another donkey, and once more we were all mounted. My cavallo being the aforesaid donkey.

From Rosario the country improved gradually and we always had enough to eat and found water and grass every day. For most of the way the trail led along the coast. One day we were obliged to make a detour from the beach to avoid the odor of a huge stranded and decaying whale. To our disgust, 100 or more wild Indians were on or around, tearing off and devouring the putrid flesh, or rolling on the sand and howling like coyotes as if in pain. It was surprising to notice the great quantity of whales' skeletons and scattered bones everywhere along this beach. The wild Indians about here are nearer brute beasts than anything in human form we had before seen or imagined. They appeared to have no houses and to live around like wolves or jack rabbits. We were told at Rosario to be on our guard as they have bows and would at night creep near our camp and shoot our horses with poisoned arrows to get their flesh to eat. Accordingly we were careful where we camped and kept watch by turns. We passed several small valleys and brooks and five or six missions in ruins and deserted, but every day we came to one or more ranches of a better kind than we had seen. At some of these we were treated kindly, at others they would neither give or sell to us. At one place there was an abundance of corn, beans and beef. We were out of food and tried to buy, but the swarthy proprietor ordered us away with insulting words. So we just quietly took what we needed and threw down to him in money a fair price for the food. We traveled early and late and as fast as possible. We felt sure that could we reach San Diego our countrymen would relieve us.

June 11th—San Diego. Once more in the dominion of the glorious Stars and Stripes. Never did I feel such a thrill as when yesterday we suddenly hove in sight of the Star-Spangled banner and knew that now we were under the protection of the flag of our beloved country. Impulsively we gave cheer upon cheer. Once again upon American soil, out of that infernal Mexico. Looking back, the past is like a horrid dream. My last entry was at San Fernando. Since then I have not had spirit to write, or any desire to keep a record—"Sufficient for the day was the evil thereof." Even now our troubles are not over. It is called 25 days' journey to San Francisco. Everything is dear and we are almost penniless, but we are among our own countrymen and will not despair. Nye and I have each a bill of exchange on San Francisco and hope we can raise money on them, but God only knows we look so like ruffians. They talk here of sickness, bloodshed and murder in the mines, but little would we seek could we hold up our heads and go on our way. My journal has got to be only a continual sad wail—I am sick of it. The incidents of this peninsula journey are engraved on my mind. They will not be forgotten. Should anything happen, let them die with me, and it will be better that my friends should not know what I have suffered. And here I shall close this narrative. Thank God, Nye has got some money. (That was the last entry in my journal.)

Our exhiliration on reaching San Diego soon gave way to a proud bashfulness, perhaps hard to explain, but when we saw the marks of civilized society, well-dressed officers, soldiers and citizens, we were ashamed of our ragged clothes and bronzed, hairy visages, and we did not at once go near them. It seems that a rumor of our party and bad condition had gone before us. We camped on the outskirts of the village near the stream. Nearby were a dozen or more large tents and the equipments of a well-furnished company, that we afterward learned was the

U.S. Boundary Survey party under Colonel John B. Weller. Further on near the barracks were many soldiers' tents. On the plaza a band was playing and we could see a company of soldiers drilling.

Among the first who spoke to us was a dragoon, an Irishman. He walked up, saying: "An how are ye, my boys? Ye've had a hard time, my poor fellows. Niver mind, now, yer among yer own countrymen." He patted me on the shoulder, and for the first time in a long while I burst into tears. He looked at my bare feet and sandals and went away. He soon came back with a new pair of soldier brogans, which he bade me to put on, saying: "Ye nade them, my poor boy, more than I do." Soon after a lad came over from the surveyor's camp and, with Mr. Weller's compliments, asked us to supper. We gladly accepted and enjoyed a square meal of pork and hard bread.

I felt strongly inclined to introduce myself to Mr. Weller, for he knew father and our family in Ohio, but knowing that he and Uncle Robert had been such bitter political opponents, somehow, and in such a forlorn guise, I could not do it. Though I know it was mean to have not told him who I was, I regretted more when afterwards I learned that one of the company, who it happened I did not meet, was a boyhood friend from Franklin, but no doubt the loss was more mine than to Bill Kinder.

Next morning Miller learned that two of his brother officers in the war were among the garrison, viz., Major Emory and Lieutenant Sweeney. We dressed up Miller and Nye the best we could and sent them over. They introduced themselves and no sooner was it known who we were and what we had suffered—the last our appearance showed without any talk—than officers, soldiers and citizens vied in loading us with such kindness as forced tears of gratitude from our eyes and smiles from our weather hardened faces. They gave us clothes, provisions and anything they had which we appeared to need. More than that, they loaned us money on no security but our word—would not even take our notes. I here record that about the first thing we did in San Francisco was to deposit that money with the house of Simmons & Hutchison, as they requested.

One day Lieutenant Sweeney invited us to dinner. We all went, proud of shoes and clothes good enough, we felt, for a king. His accomplished lady presided at a table which seemed to us to be loaded with every delicacy that could be wished for. Both the lieutenant and his good wife treated us during our stay as if we had been their own brothers. Never was attention more gratefully appreciated. We all vowed that this disinterested kindness should be a life-long lesson of humanity and that we, too, would ever try to benefit any poor waif who might fall in our way. May God bless these kind people.

We stayed in San Diego five days, our horses fattening on an open field of wild oats nearby. The morning of the fifteenth we bade adieu to our good friends and pushed on, well equipped and in better spirits than for months before.

From thence to San Francisco our journey was comparatively a pleasure jaunt. At last we had found and entered that California we had read of—with hills covered with wild oats, grassy plains, valley brooks and herds of countless cattle and horses. Some things were getting dear, but with us the main thing was beef and plenty of it. At almost every ranch there would be hanging quarters of fresh beef. When we asked to buy they would hand us a knife and tell us to cut all we wanted. They preferred to give us meat, rather than we should shoot down a steer as travellers generally did; because then they lost the hide which was the main value of the animal. We passed places where apparently thousands of cattle had been killed and were told that all but the hides and horns were thrown away.

Three days' ride brought us to San Luis Rey, a large brick and adobe mission. The San Diego mission and all to the north of that place were founded by Franciscans under the lead of Padre Junipero Serra. When the Spanish government suppressed the Jesuit missions in Lower California they were turned over to the Franciscans, but it appears that they took little interest in the Jesuit enterprise and allowed the missions in the desert abaho to perish. The mission buildings in Lower California are generally built of stone and mortar and are far more substantial than those we saw in the Alta, which are mostly constructed of adobe plastered. The mission of San Luis Rey was occupied by a company of U.S. dragoons.

A few days more over plains literally covered with innumerable fat cattle and horses found us camped by the river side in the environs of the beautiful Pueblo de Los Angeles, or City of the Angels. According to our late experience, it was truly named, and seemed to us a very paradise of fruits and flowers. From there we turned off to the coast by way of San Buena, Ventura, Santa Barbara, San Luis Obispo, Paso Robles Springs, San Miguel and San Jose. We pressed forward with all speed, trading horses and pistols for fresh animals and, having made 700 miles from San Diego in 22 days, entered San Francisco on the 6th day of July.

The *Mary Frances* had arrived on the 3rd of May. Our friends on her had long since given us up as lost. They met us with open arms and gave us a grand banquet as a rejoicing for our safety.

Now, in conclusion! It is only your frequent solicitation, my friends, that induces me to send you this narrative. I had hoped that soon after this time I should see you all and have the pleasure of telling these things. I think I could have varnished the story in a manner that would make it more interesting, but circumstances make it uncertain when I shall be with you again. So in the intervals of business I have written off this hasty sketch. I am well aware that it has many imperfections in composition which perhaps I might improve could I take time, but, knowing it will be read by no harsh judges, I send it to you, all imperfect as it is, with this understanding that it is for your perusal and your's alone.'

W.C.S. Smith.

Marysville, January 24th, 1851.

———

SUPPLEMENT — 1888

So much has been written descriptive of the early days of San Francisco that the field is overworked. So I will briefly mention that we came in from the mission by a trail over the sand hills and through thick chapparal. We found the first houses and tents at the corner of Kearney and Clay Streets. Around Portsmouth Square were several adobe buildings. A frame hotel, the Parker House, was being built on the northeast corner of Kearney and Clay. On Washington Street to Montgomery and on Montgomery to Jackson Street were occasional canvass houses and some scattering houses around the foot of Telegraph Hill. On Montgomery, corner of Jackson, was a rough wooden bridge over an arm of the bay. The beach shore ran in a crescent southeast from this bridge by what is now Sansome and Battery Streets. The two large redwood warehouses of Simmons & Hutchinson and Prime, Ward & King stood on the beach. Northward from the bridge the shore line extended east to what was called Clarks Point. Many ships were anchored a quarter of a mile or more from shore, and of these a large number were deserted — officers and crew gone to the mines.

52

Apparently there were in San Francisco people of every nation in the world, and a reckless, confused state of things beyond any description. We soon got tired of the confusion. July 12th Nye and I sailed in an open boat for Sacramento. Miller and B. had gone several days before with a company to the mines. We were three days going up the river, which was filled with schooners and boats of every kind, loaded with people who like ourselves were bound for the mines.

It had been my opinion that no mosquito in the world could compete in size and execution with the animal bred in the Mississippi bottoms, but they could not "hold a candle" to those we encountered on the Sacramento River and slough. They did not cease from their work day or night, and they went for blood. One night we tried to camp and built a big smudge, but it was no use. They drove us to the boat. Strange to say, and to our joy and relief, in the town of Sacramento there was not a mosquito.

Sacramento was filled with a motley crowd of adventurers. The morning of our arrival we walked out to Sutter's Fort for breakfast, and to see the faces and be waited on by the McClellan girls who, with their mother, were then the only white women in the country around. It was no ordinary privilege in those days to look at a woman.

At Sacramento we found Gardner and several others of our company. In a day or two we arranged with a man with an ox team to haul our provisions and blankets to Roses Bar on the Yuba River, about 100 miles. We were four days on the road. At Roses Bar we found several of the Frenchmen, who greeted us most cordially. They had been there a month and had washed out a good deal of gold. With their instruction we were soon at work and getting gold ourselves.

In about ten days Nye and I, with two others, went on a prospecting trip of a week or more up Deer Creek, up to and beyond the site of the present town of Nevada. There were no white men on the creek, but plenty of wild Indians. We found gold everywhere, but, as we thought, not enough to pay. It was then considered poor diggings that did not pay at least a dollar to the pan. We did not know that we were scratching over what soon after proved to be the richest mines in the country.

We worked at Roses Bar about 12 days longer, making about two ounces a day each. Everyone thought there must be a place up the river very rich, from where the gold came, because ascending the river the gold steadily grew coarser. So one day Nye, two of the Frenchmen and I packed a horse and started up. Also we each packed on our own backs about 50 pounds. We traveled on up the mountains for about a week. The weather was very hot, but we enjoyed the tramp. There were frequent springs of ice cold water. As we came to the higher mountains we were amazed at the immense size and height of the trees. When we reached the summit of the divide, at what was called Slate Range, we turned our horse loose to care for himself and went down the side of the canyon, so steep we could only travel by clinging to bushes, for about a mile to the North Yuba River, opposite to the mouth of Slate Creek. It was a dark and gloomy gorge, into which the sun shone only a few hours in the day. Here we found an Oregon man and a boy. They had about 25 pounds of coarse gold in a buckskin bag, which they had washed in a week with a rocker made from half a hollow log. He said he thought there were better diggings higher up the river, and offered us his claim for $400. We bought it and washed the gold to pay him in less than a day. The ground was sand and gravel on a slate bed, from which we washed a pint or more of clean, coarse gold each day. Our machine was the said half of a hollow log resting on two cross logs, a crooked manzanita stick lashed around for a handle and a sloping screen of split sticks at one end. The dirt had to be carried about 100 feet. From a canvass sailor bag, two poles and a cross stick I made a hand-barrow.

In the forenoon we would dig and carry to the rocker by the river about 10 or 12 loads and in the afternoon wash it out. One would keep the rocker rocking, another lay the gravel on the screen and a third one of us throw water on the gravel with a tin pan fastened on a forked stick. Our rude machine was so imperfect that we saved no gold finer than bird shot. I am sure we lost half.

Soon after we came a store was started on the top of the ridge. As our provisions gave out one of us would go up twice or three times a week for food. It took a whole day of hard work to climb the mountain and come back. We paid in gold dust at $16.00 per ounce! Per pound of flour, $1.00; pork or bacon, $2.00; sugar, $2.00; crackers, $1.00; saleratus, $16.00, and vinegar, $8.00 for a pint bottle.

Above our camp on each side of the river the slate stood up in high, broken projections on edge at an angle of perhaps 45 degrees. It was easily split in thin sheets and between these sheets was more or less fine gold. One day with a knife and pan I scraped and washed out in a few hours over $400.

Just below our camp the river plunged with a wild roar over a precipice into a dark, inaccessible canyon.

Other people soon followed us and in a few weeks a hundred or more were working near by. In a camp close to us several who had come around the Horn died from scurvy, caused by living so long on salt food. It was a horrid death. There was a kind of wild lettuce on the hillsides and water cress which we ate to keep off the disease.

About the middle of September Mr. Perret, the chief man of the French party, came up from Sacramento, where he had his office, to see how we were doing. We divided our gold by measure with a tin cup and each had about $5,000. We sent it to Sacramento by Mr. Perret to take care of for us. Nye went back with Mr. Perret. A few days afterward I was badly hurt when rolling a large rock and laid in camp for two weeks before I had strength to get out of the canyon with assistance. I went down to Roses Bar with a returning pack train; from there to Sacramento in a mule wagon, and arrived in pretty bad condition.

I stopped with Mr. Perret at the Hotel de France and there made several pleasant acquaintances, among others Dr. John F. Morse, a noted physician and Odd Fellow. One evening about ten days after my arrival I was taken with a chill, became unconscious and remained so several days. To Dr. Morse I owe my life. He took me to his office and nursed me like a brother. He said I was fairly broken down. About this time my fellow traveler B. died in San Francisco from the same fever.

The French company of which Mr. Perret was chief, in addition to their expedition by the way of Mexico, sent out the ship *Pacific* with passengers and a miscellaneous cargo of supplies, which were stored in a large tent on I Street near the levee. They had mining and trading camps at Mormon Island, Auburn and other places, and schooners plying to San Francisco.

Among their outfit was machinery for a steam gang sawmill. Lumber in Sacramento was $500 per 1000 feet, mostly brought from the states. As I had some practical knowledge of woodcraft, Mr. Perret employed me to find a location and superintend the erection of a mill. I was to have $400 a month and 10 per cent of the net sales of lumber. In that view I went in an eight-oared iron sailboat up the Sacramento and Feather rivers to about twenty miles above the mouth of the Yuba. With me were eight others, one a millwright, a Scotchman from Oregon by the name of Fenton. We were well equipped. A good boat, a fine tent and plenty of provisions. One night we stayed at Hock Farm, Captain Sutter's ranch. The captain was much interested in our enterprise and was very kind and hospitable. Another night far up Feather River we were interviewed by a grizzly and the bear held all the honors.

We had camped on a sandy spit between the river and a bayou. It was covered with a dense growth of willows, except a clear spot about 100 feet from the shore, where we pitched our tent, made a fire and cooked supper, after which all went to bed except Fenton and I. We were sitting by the low fire smoking. The night was intensely dark. Suddenly we heard something crashing through the brush across the bayou and into the water, puffing and grunting. Fento was an old Hudson Bay Company trapper and recognized that it was a bear. He sprang up, saying "get into the tent quick." We did, and told the boys, "There is a bear in camp."

We grasped our guns, but, as Fenton charged us, kept still and waited. Soon we heard him knocking our tin plates around. Presently he found our jug of molasses which he licked and licked and rolled around in the sand. Now and then he would stop and come close to the tent. We could hear him breathe. We wanted to shoot at him in the dark, but Fenton would not let us do so, as he said it would surely result in some of us being killed. So we nine men sat all that long night listening to that bear. Before daylight he went away, leaving our provisions badly demoralized. We could see his footprints in the sand a foot long. We felt mean and cowardly about it, but I expect the old Scotchman's prudent discretion was the better part of valor.

Returning down Feather River, we went up the Yuba to Nye's Ranch, now Marysville. This ranch was only one adobe house. We there left the boat and went afoot up the Yuba some twenty miles, where we selected a site for the mill. This was about the 1st of December, and very stormy weather. When we got back to Nye's Ranch almost the whole country was under water. A great many emigrants from across the plains were camped around in wagons and tents. Land travel was impossible. In consequence food, except beef, was scarce and dear.

On the ranch were many Spanish cattle, said to be 10,000 head. The grant had lately been sold by Michael Nye to Covilland, Ramirez and Sampson. They had a kind of store in one end of the adobe, where they sold a few articles of common necessity at fabulous prices. At Sacramento flour was $12.00 per barrel; here they sold it for $1.00 per pound.

On our return down the river we had as a passenger in our boat an old one-eyed Frenchman by the name of Sicard. The past history and final career of this man was typical and romantic. He had been a common sailor in the French navy. Had an eye knocked out in the battle of Navarino with the Turks. Twenty years before he deserted from a man-o'-war on this coast. Lived with an Indian tribe, of which he got to be chief. When gold was discovered he took his tribe to the Yuba at what is known as Sicard's Bar and set them to work. Now for the first time he was going to the city to invest the proceeds of the Indians' labor, $60,000 in gold dust, which he had with him in buckskin bags. Two years afterward I met the old fellow on Parks Bar, where he was again living with the Indians and in great poverty. Partly from him and others I learned what he did with all his gold.

In San Francisco he fell in with some countrymen and had a good time. They persuaded him that he, who had sailed so long in the forecastle, should now be an officer and called him commodore. To carry out the idea he bought a large ship, fitted her out with abundant stores, shipped a crew, took as free passengers a lot of boon friends, male and female, and as captain in command sailed away to China, the islands of the Pacific, Australia, Valparaiso, etc., had a grand old spree and got back to San Francisco in about a year, where the vessel was attached and sold on bottomry bonds, and the old man left without a dollar.

After reporting to Mr. Perret, he decided to defer the mill business until spring. I happened to find a lot of 300 barrels of flour stored on a vessel and offered for $12.00 per barrel. I thought it would be a good speculation to buy it, and asked Mr. Perret for my gold. He told me he had presumed upon the liberty of friendship and used it, but would give it to me in a few days. Several weeks passed and on various plausible excuses he did not pay me. I had much reason to think Mr. Perret as honest as he was generous, but was quite importunate as I wanted to secure the flour. On the morning of December 24th he said he would settle with me at 10 o'clock next day at his office and invited me to a banquet he would give that evening at the Hotel de France. That was a perfect high jinks. There were about twenty guests, mostly Frenchmen. Among the guests I remember were Major Redding, Captain Sutter and Sam Brannan. Champagne and other wines flowed freely. They made speeches, gave toasts, sang the Marsellaise and other songs, pitched their wine glasses over their shoulders and had a jolly time. Mr. Perret was the leader in all the fun.

When we broke up about midnight Mr. Perret shook hands and said to me, "Now be sure and come around in the morning." I went, but found the office locked. I waited around an hour or more, then peered into a window of a rear room where he slept and could see him on the bed. I pounded on the window but could not rouse him. I then went for one of the company. We forced the door, and there on the bed, nicely dressed, a pistol in his hand and the top of his head blown off, lay Mr. Perret, and in a stove were the burnt remnants of all his books and accounts.

Next week flour was selling for $100 per barrel. Thus I was

out my own $5,000 gold dust and a certain profit on the flour I had bargained for of over $26,000. I had nothing to show that this money was owing except Mr. Perret's admission in presence of mutual friends that he had my gold dust. There was no lawyer for me to appeal to. So, acting on the advice and with the assistance of these friends, I at once took possession of a quantity of provisions and merchandise stored in the tent I have referred to and removed them to the barque *Orb*, and also appropriated the iron boat I have spoken of. I loaded the boat with about two tons of provisions and started for Nye's Landing. Was two days going. When the wind served I sailed, at other times some sailors who were working their passage rowed. I sold my load at once to the store for a big price.

Mr. Covilland mentioned that they would lay out a town if they had a surveyor. I told him of a Mr. Plongeon in Sacramento who I would try to bring next trip. I made another round trip in five days, bringing the surveyor. The next time I came back Mr. Plongeon asked me to help him lay out the streets of the town, which I did for several days.

Mr. Plongeon made his own instrument ingeniously of two sticks crossed at right angles and set on a staff, and at each end of the sticks an upright peg with a slit and a horsehair. Crude as this instrument was, I think the survey of Marysville was a good piece of work. This same Mr. Plongeon is the man now so distinguished for archeological researches and discoveries in Central America.

I bought a lot and built a canvass house and, in company with two young men from New York, opened a store for the sale of general merchandise. We did a good business; made money fast. One evening the proprietors called a citizens' meeting to name the town. We called it Marysville after Mrs. Covilland, one of the very few women there.

I made a number more trips in the boat for goods. There

was a strange inconsistency in prices. There was scarcely a limit to the price of a needed article when in the right shape for use, while many valuable staple goods could not be given away. For instance, ground coffee in one-pound tin cans was worth $12 per pound. While choice green Java and Rio in sacks were used to fill holes in the streets. Time was too precious to spend in burning and grinding coffee.

The commonest laborer asked and got $16 per day. It was the same with saleratus, one-pound packages sold for $16. Yet one day at an auction in Sacramento I bought two barrels, about 800 pounds, of saleratus for $1.00 the lot.

The auctioneer said to me, "Now, you, take that stuff away or I will have it moved at your expense." I replied, "Don't you fret." I had an idea. I knew where I could get for a trifle a lot of small tin cans that some fool had sent out from New York to pack gold dust in, I took the saleratus and cans to Marysville, got some Indians to pack it, and jobbed the whole lot off at from $5 to $12 per pound.

One day it was found that some fellow had bought up all the tacks in California. Canvass houses could not be built without tacks. So up they went from 10 cents a paper to 1 cent a tack.

In the winter I had seen tons of plug tobacco in cases, bundles of mowing scythes, crowbars, etc., thrown down in the streets of San Francisco for walks and crossings. In the spring we had several calls for scythes. The next time I went to San Francisco I bought a quantity of scythes and sneaths, pitchforks and whetstones for almost nothing, took them to Marysville and sold the scythes quick for $25 each.

Among other things I had shipped from New York around the Horn was a small grindstone. The day I unpacked it in Marysville I sold it for $150. It was the only grindstone there, and the man who bought it made a small fortune grinding tools for others.

We did a good business that winter. Our store was a rude structure, only canvass over poles and a ground floor, yet it was as good as any of our neighbors had. My bed was my blankets on a pile of boxes. I had camped on the ground so long that it was no hardship but a privilege to sleep on dry boards. There were many houses of wood or sheet iron sent out from the east ready made to set up. A friend who owned an iron house with a floor offered me a place to spread my blankets. One night it rained hard and the way that house roared inside would discount ten bass drums. I did not try to sleep there any more.

In the spring we bought in Sacramento a Philadelphia-made two-story frame house 25 by 50 feet built in panels. I do not remember how many thousands of dollars it cost to set that house up in Marysville, but it was a sum that would now seem fabulous. However, it was a good investment for business, and added to our comfort. It was no small matter to have a good roof overhead and a floor underfoot. The upper story we divided with cloth into small sleeping rooms for our customers from the mines. In those days everyone took with them and slept in their own blankets. In my trips to Sacramento and San Francisco I always carried my blankets along. There was a reason well known to pioneers which made public beds unpopular.

The town grew rapidly. In a few months many streets and blocks were well defined by houses, and there was a population of several thousand, but the good class of people of the first immigration was soon outnumbered by hordes of gamblers and ruffians who poured in from every country on the globe. Notorious among whom were many of the Botany Bay convicts from Sydney.

In the beginning there was little occasion for laws or courts. As a general thing, all honestly minded their own business, and there was peace and security. Anyone who violated another's rights got speedy justice. Horse thieves were hung on sight. But that Utopian condition was fast passing away. So as a matter of necessity a meeting of citizens was held and measures taken to organize a town government. A good ticket for town officers was nominated. The gamblers and roughs also put up a ticket of their own kind, and at the election they held the polls at the point of the pistol.

As I was about to offer my vote the notorious Irish shoulder striker, "Yankee Sullivan," grasped me by the arm, saying, "Here, you, take a walk. You can't vote here." I walked. I did not care to be beaten or killed. Thus they elected their ticket, legalized missrule and lawlessness, and we were "hoist with our own petard."

During that year of 1850 shootings and murder were of almost daily occurrence. One gambler, Charley Corey, to my knowledge killed six men in four months. I saw him kill two. Will mention here that in 1854 the San Francisco Vigilante Committee hung this Corey and caught Yankee Sullivan to hang him, but he cheated the rope by suicide.

In all the towns the gambling saloons were the finest buildings, and in the best locations. Each saloon tried to rival the others in music, vocal and instrumental, which did not cease by day and hardly by night. The interior of these places was furnished regardless of expense with carpets, chairs, sofas, paintings, books and everything to comfort or attract. It was no wonder that almost everyone went to these saloons evenings. There were no other comfortable places where one could go. They were a kind of exchange where people met to do business, to meet others, and to look for friends.

Many went to these places who never gambled. The temptation to gamble was to many irresistible, no matter what had been their former life or profession. In no way could money be got so easily as by winning it from fellows just from the mines with long bags of easily gotten gold dust, and who were only too anxious to "fight the tiger." Among these regular gamblers were many men of most respectable antecedents. Even church elders and ministers of the gospel—men whose eastern friends would have been shocked to know the unvarnished facts.

There was a constant and increasing excitement created by reports of diggings high up in the mountains, rich beyond anything before known. It was not all rumor. Two sailors brought in a nugget of pure gold weighing 30 pounds. I had it in my store over night. They said there was plenty more where that came from, but the place was their secret. Another man who brought down a large quantity of gold reported that he had found a lake somewhere at the head of the rivers on whose shore clean gold could be scraped up by the pound, and that lake was his secret.

Now the great idea was to reach this gold lake before others. Parties who thought they had the secret would slip off quietly by night and try to hide their trail. No one doubted that an El Dorado lay hidden among the high, snowy mountain peaks. We were like the rest.

Early in May, soon as it was thought the weather and snow in the mountains would permit travel, we fitted out a pack train of ten mules, loaded with provisions, with the idea that if we did not find a gold mine we could do some trading. I was chosen to take charge of the venture. I had three men in company to assist. We followed the divide north of the Yuba to Grass Valley at the head of the south fork of the Feather River, thence to Onion Valley and the mouth of Nelson Creek, a branch of the middle fork of the Feather. In places we passed over snow 50 feet and more in depth. This depth we measured by dropping a line down by the side of trees. Around the larger trees was a melted circle down to the earth. We thought this melting was caused by heat from the trees.

In several places, particularly on Nelson Creek, we found good diggings, but did not find that gold lake. That was somewhere still further on. How much further was a case of "quien sabe." It was awful cold and my mules were nearly starved. I sold my goods at a handsome profit and was satisfied to go back to the valley, at least for the present, but fully determined to see more of the country among these high, wild mountains at no distant day.

One of my best friends and a good customer at our store was Captain Estabrook, who brought out the ship *Pacific*. He was owner of what was known as "Charley's Ranch," 16 miles up the Feather River road, where he had a store and a popular roadside house of entertainment. The captain was always urging me to visit him and several times I rode up in the evening and back in the early morning. The road along the river bank was good and pleasant. I had a large, splendid saddle mule. The captain was a noble, whole-souled gentleman. I enjoyed those rides and visits.

One morning I started from the ranch at daybreak and had an adventure. I was galloping merrily along the narrow, winding road at a place where trees and brush grew thick on each side, when suddenly we almost ran into a huge grizzly sitting up in the track. With a snort my mule made a right-angled jump that almost pitched me from his back into the bear's paws, and broke off through the brush with a rush. I thought the bushes and vines would pull me off, but I held on. I have never been sure which of us was the most frightened, the mule, the bear or I.

At that time bears were plenty in the river bottoms and killed many cattle and calves. Generally they would run from men, but not always. Two young men friends of mine had made a profitable business of hunting bear and deer. One morning they left my store on a hunt and never came back.

Months after a broken gun, fragments of clothing and a few bones found in the tules near the Buttes revealed their fate.

That summer many people died from cholera. Three died in my store. In some cases persons would be taken sick and die in a few minutes.

Our business was good but for sufficient reasons I was not satisfied with my partners and sold out to them in the spring of '51. I was the more willing to sell because I wanted to try my fortune in the mines again.

Soon after I formed a partnership with a Mr. Sherman for the purpose of trading, prospecting and mining, in which view we loaded ten mules and struck off up the mountains. We had a Mexican to help, but packing is hard work. In following a train, when not in mud or snow, one is in a cloud of hot dust. Every little while a pack will turn or come loose, or a mule stampede. And then one must constantly watch these old pack mules, they are fond of sugar or flour and miss not chance to bite open a sack. We were always tired enough to be glad to spread our blankets on the ground and sleep. When we got up in the snow we would at night build a house of poles and fir boughs and would lay on the ground, shingle fashion to sleep on, these fir boughs, which made a bed equal to a spring mattress. One without trial would hardly believe how warm and dry these houses were, or how soon one could be built. I remember one morning when our camp was entirely buried in new snow that we were quite comfortable.

Our route was nearly the same I took the year before. At Independence Bar on Nelson Creek we left part of our cargo in a store to be sold. Thence we crossed the middle fork of the Feather River at the mouth of Nelson Creek and over the mountains to American Valley. This valley lies on a stream flowing northwest into the north fork of the Feather. Here we fell in with a company of seven Marysville friends, who like us were prospectors, and a few days after together we struck good diggings at a place known as Humbug Gulch. We agreed to join forces and, while some worked this mine, a part of the company should go further on and hunt for Gold Lake or other rich diggings.

As a headquarters we built a good shanty near the bank of a beautiful little creek and fixed things comfortable. There was fine pasture in the valleys on which the Mexican herded all our animals. In American Valley was a band of cattle and a ranch where they sold beef. We bought a quarter of beef and hung it on a tree near the camp, and that same night a grizzly carried it off. Next morning we followed his trail a long distance into a rocky canyon, and there made meat of him. I will here record that we soon all agreed that bear meat was a miserable substitute for beef. We got very tired of it.

To work our mine to advantage we brought water from the creek into the head of the gulch by a ditch a mile or more in length. There was a species of white cedar which split well into boards with which we built sluice boxes.

The gold was in the surface soil of the gulch and the hillsides and was in sprays with more or less small pieces of white quartz attached. It evidently came from a decomposing vein somewhere up the mountain side. We did a great deal of work trying to find that vein, but without success. Years afterward others more fortunate did find close by where we had dug a quartz vein that proved to be and yet is one of the richest in California.

In the latter part of June five of us started on the intended prospecting trip. We struck the middle fork at the mouth of Jamison Creek and followed it up through the summit ridge of the mountains by an easy pass into what is now called Beckwith Valley. We were surprised to find so good and practicable a passage way through these high and rugged mountains. I have since often wondered why the C.P.R.R. was not built through this pass, which is so much lower and easier than the present road. The difference in altitude is quite 4000 feet. The best natural road over the Sierra Nevada is by way of Bidwells Bar, North Feather, American Valley and Beckwith Pass.

Beckwith Valley is about 20 miles long and from two to four miles wide. It is level and fertile and, as we saw it, was covered with a beautiful growth of tall grass and was full of deer, antelope and bear. The surrounding mountain sides were covered with heavy forest and points of timber groves extended from the margin out in the valley, with grassy intervals through which ran clear, cold brooks. These groves were full of grouse and, indeed, we were seldom out of sight or shooting distance of some kind of game. Every day was interesting and enjoyable.

Now, at the risk of being thought too numerous with bear stories, I must here tell just one more: One evening just before going into camp, as we rode along the edge of the valley, we saw at a short distance out from a point of timber two bears industriously scratching up the ground, hunting for mice as is their habit. They did not see us, and one of my companions, Jesse D., proposed to me that we try to get a shot at them. So after camping we went cautiously through the timber towards them. The bears were about 200 yards beyond the last tree. This was a tamarack covered with brush to the ground. Luckily we examined the tree, thinking we might possibly need to use it. From there we crawled in the high grass about half way to where the bears were yet scratching, then rose up and fired. They were both hit, but, instead of falling, looked up and started for us. We dropped our empty guns and broke for the tree at our very best gait. We made it, but were only out of their reach with not one moment to spare. They reared up against the tree and snarled and growled around for ten or fifteen minutes and then to our relief left. It seemed to us a long time, for the tree was small and we were not sure but they would get us. When we got back to camp and Jesse was telling how I outran him, one of the boys asked him what his thoughts were when the bears were so close on him, he said: "Well, I thought Smith was a mighty good runner, but a d——d slow climber."

Toward the southern end the valley forks like the letter Y. Both forks are separated from the Truckee River at their southern end by a low timbered divide. The western fork is now called Sierra Valley. We went down the east fork to the river and then followed the river up some distance to where it flowed out of a round lake, to which we gave the name of "Silver Lake." Don't know what it is called now. This is a beautiful sheet of crystal clear water about half a mile across and surrounded on all sides but the east by high, snow-clad mountains. We climbed with difficulty a high peak on the west side, from which we could see the branches of the Yuba River and the country for many miles around spread out like a map. The last thousand feet or more of our climb was over hard snow, which apparently had been there from the beginning of time.

We returned by way of Sierra Valley, and from there went west over the summit ridge to the heads of Jamison and Canon creeks, which, respectively, flow into the Yuba and Feather. The country was very rugged and broken and in addition we encountered a violent snowstorm. We were quite bewildered and with difficulty could keep a course or make any progress, but fortunately before night came on we found a way down a long steep incline into a little sheltered valley and a comfortable camp.

From there we followed down Jamison Creek to the foot of a high, isolated peak called Mount 76, where we found several persons mining in the creek. That is quite cold country. I remember that night I set a cup of water at my head and in the morning it was frozen solid. The next day was the Fourth of July. We decided to celebrate the day by scaling the mountain. We found it a hard climb. This is the highest peak in that neighborhood, except perhaps Pilot Peak between Onion Valley and Nelson Creek. The view from the summit was grand. We stood on the frozen snow and gave three rousing cheers for the day.

Coming down we walked and slid over snow for several thousand feet. When about half way down the western side of the mountain we stopped to examine a great vein of white quartz which stood up like a wall 40 or 50 feet high. We had noticed this white object before when many miles distant on our way out. Now we were much interested to find that this semi-transparent quartz was full of visible fine gold. Apparently there were millions there, but the rock was exceedingly hard and so far as any way we then knew of it would cost all or more than the gold to get it out.

Soon after some parties I knew undertook to work it, but after sinking much money gave it up. Some years afterward when a better way of reducing such quartz had been discovered another company by an improved process proved that this same ledge was immensely valuable.

We did a great deal of digging and prospecting on our trip and found gold in many places, but no diggings more promising than where we were working.

On return to the camp on Humbug it was necessary to send a train down to Marysville for supplies and merchandise. As my business required me to go there soon, I volunteered for the service. Three of us went down with twenty mules, which we loaded at Marysville and drove back to our camp without much incident. In the valley and foothills it was fearfully hot and dusty and we were glad when back again to the cool waters and breezes of the mountains.

On our return we found Nelson Creek roaring high, and not fordable. Caused by melting of snow. An enterprising fellow had fallen a large, tall pine tree across the creek near the mouth and established a toll bridge of a primitive and most rickety kind. It was only a few feet wide, with no railing, and sprung and swayed back and forth. One of our mules loaded with pork capsized and went over and down about fifty feet into the raging flood and out in Feather River. We thought he was a dead, drowned mule sure, but to our surprise he fetched up on a bar a half mile below and we got him and the pork out all right.

Index

COLOPHON

The William C.S. Smith A JOURNEY TO CALIFORNIA IN 1849 *was printed in the workshop of Glen Adams, which is located in the sleepy country village of Fairfield, southern Spokane County, in Washington State. The text is set in fourteen point Baskerville with running heads and page numbers in twenty-four point Mahogany Script. The title page is set in Baskerville Bold. The title page border is in No. 500 hand set border type somewhat reduced. This was purchased a quarter of a century ago from the Stephenson, Blake Foundry in Sheffield, England. The text was keyboarded by Sharyn Brown using a model 2750 Editwriter computer photosetter. Camera-darkroom work was by Evelyn Foote Clausen using a model 660C DS camera. The film was stripped and printing plates made by Millie Ferger. The sheets were printed by Robert LaTendresse using a 28 inch KORS Heidelberg press. Folding was by Garry Adams using a 22x28 three stage Baum folding machine. Assembly was by the Ye Galleon crew. The index was done by Edward J. Kowrach of Veradale, Washington. Paper stock is seventy pound Baronet Matte. Binding is by Willem Bosch of Oakesdale, Washington assisted by Geritt Bosch and Bill Harnois. This was a fun project. We had no special difficulty with the work.*